The Rhymers

Mubble Pup's Mubble Twisters

Written and illustrated by
Andrew Buller

The wise wind whistled...

www.meettherhymers.com

www.andrewbuller.com

Dedicated to anyone
who has ever got mubbled up.

Believe in yourself.
Celebrate who you are.
Be amazing!

Just like Mubble Pup.

Early learning experts value the use of tongue twisters
to aid speech and language development.

The Rhymers series provide a wonderful way to learn
through each of their fun, engaging, colourful books.

How many times can you
spot Mubble Pup in this book too?

Andrew Buller Books

First published in Great Britain in 2016

Text & illustration copyright © 2016 Andrew Buller

I acknowledge the help of Malcolm Buller in the creative development of this book.

ISBN: 978-1534672789

"I'm muddy Mubble Pup.

Dash's crashed dishes.

Giggle and Jiggle juggle

Whizzy wonders

why Izzy's wands
wander.

Kick kicks while quickly quacking,

"Quack, Queck, Quick, Quock, Quuck!"

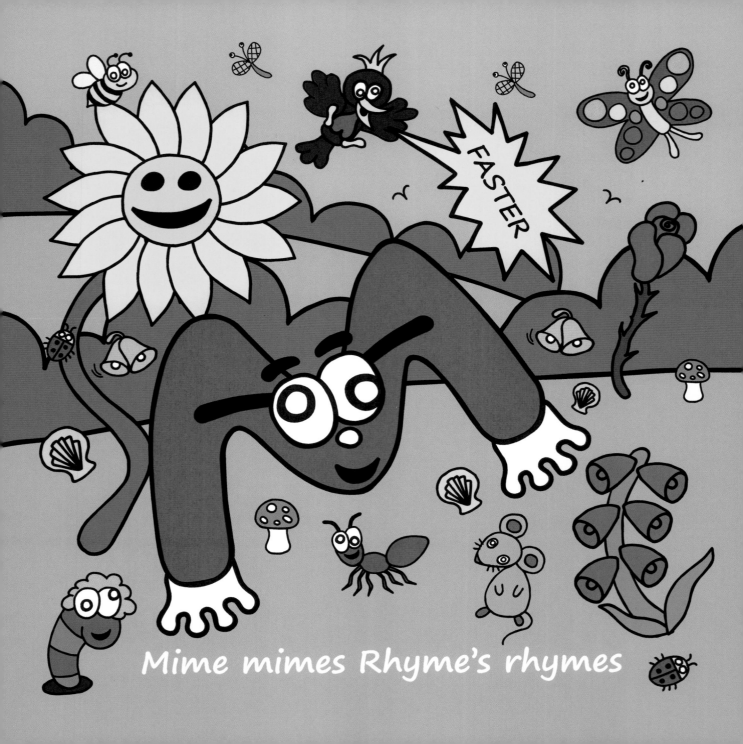

Mime mimes Rhyme's rhymes

as Rhyme rhymes Mime's mimes.

so Nap's not napping.

Pop and Top's pickled, peppered bubbles popped.

Vroom zooms
around the moon,

while Zoom vrooms
round Rocket Room.

"I'm marvellous Mubble Pup!

I've mubble-muddled,
muddle-mubbled,
muddled all you Rhymers up!"

Lots and lots of spots to spot!

 Peter Parrot picked a
pickled, peppered pickle.

 Seagulls singing seashell songs
along the seashell shore.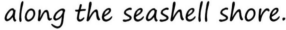

 How much wood would Woodpecker peck
if Woodpecker could peck wood?

  Flying, fleeing frogs fly
faster, faster, faster.

  Wig Worm wiggles while Wag Worm waggles.

 Crazy Daisy drives Daisy crazy.

 Robin's bob, bob, bobbing with her bob, bob, bobbing robins.

 Sneaky Snail leaves seven slippery trails.

 Many, many Mubble Pups mean many, many muddle ups!

So many Rhymers books to collect...

Rhyming alphabet stories
for the capital Rhymers
and little letter Rising Rhymers

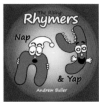

Stories for loveable Mubble Pup
and little Mubble Puppy,
The Rhymers' dizzy-leg-sick dog

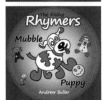

Early learning books teaching the
alphabet, numbers, colours, shapes
and more

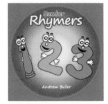

Colouring storybooks
and puzzle books full of mazes,
wordsearches, games and more

www.meettherhymers.com   www.andrewbuller.com

Printed in Great Britain
by Amazon